The Lives of Owls
A PRISMATIC Coloring Book

Jada Fitch

The Lives of Owls
A PRISMATIC Coloring Book

ISBN: 1545427844
ISBN-13: 978-1545427842

The Lives of Owls

A book that will rhyme

So take out your crayons

It's coloring time

A Kenyan evening

Just before sunset

An **Abyssinian Owl**

Has not woken up yet

Great Horned Owl Chicks

Come out in the spring

They play in the undergrowth

And swing upon a swing

The **Boobook** is proud

A fine hunter is he

He has caught a tree snake

Atop of a tree

A **Tawny Owl** visits late

A lovely cottage on

A quiet acre in the woods

With very well kept lawn

An **African Grass Owl**

Perched up on a fence

Watches over farmland

Waiting for rodents

The **Pels Fishing Owl**

Always stays alert

Never scares the fish away

He's quiet and inert

Eagle Owl took a pocket watch

Committing the perfect crime

It matches with his eye color

Though he cannot read time

Behold, above, the **Saw-whet**!

He quickly plummets down

And to his furry victim

The biggest fright around!

This old **Barn Owl**

Won't follow the script

Instead of a Barn

He haunts a crypt

A **Great Horned Owl** rests

As he travels under stars

He has stopped at a bike

And holds the handlebars

This **Short-eared Owl** has

An interesting ploy

When he can't find a dinner

He takes himself a toy

The **Great Gray Owl** is still

But she is not at rest

She's protecting her offspring

By hiding in her nest

Owls of North America

Unique and diverse

Learn more about them

Study and immerse

A Long-whiskered Owlet

Hunts among fungi

He would eat a mushroom

But he finds them rather spongy

A Blakistons Fish Owl

Prepares to dine

He will not be thwarted

By a sneaking feline

Little Owl, where are you going?

When will you be back?

What sort of thing have you found

To put it that backpack?

These **Burrowing owls**

Won't find themselves needing

When they are not digging

They're always reading

A Spectacled Owl thinks

Himself quite awesome

Try telling that to

A little Mouse Opossum

Do owls fantasize?

I imagine that they might

Dream during daytime

And daydream at night

This **African Scops Owl**

has lost his left eye

His vision is poor,

But he can still fly

A **Morepork Owl** makes a catch,

A big Huhu Beetle

The beetle thinks it bad form

The owl thinks it regal

Normal folks think it strange

Others find it weird

That wizards from the forest

Keeps **Elf Owls** in their beard

The **Pygmy Owl** is at it still

Agitated, queasy

He thought he might author a book

But writing it ain't easy

The owl is grand!

A master of skies!

A symbol of night

Intelligent and wise

How many owls would you need

How many would it take

To have so many owls

That this old tree limb would break?

"None shall pass this passageway!"

Says a **Spotted Owl** from the gate

"The Castle's closed to castle guests,

The hour... much too late"

This little **Barred Owl**

Might need a cheer up

He can't find a mouse

And doesn't like syrup

This owl stalks a Harvest Mouse

Watches through wide eyes

Though it would seem his appetite

Is bigger than his size

Screech Owl Families

Are close, it's widely known

They're always tight together

And never sleep alone

These **Southern White-faced Owls**

Have made home in a strange place

Most owls would find it lacking

To live inside a vase

This owl nests in a globe

On an old forgotten shelf

No need to tell her of the world

She's seen it all herself

A hungry **Snowy Owl**

Hunts for a mouse

Using light from the moon

And glow from the lighthouse

A
PRISMATIC
COLORING BOOK

Visit us:

www.facebook.com/PRISMATICBooks

JADA FITCH
ILLUSTRATION

Jada Fitch is an illustrator living in Portland, Maine. Her work can be found everywhere from bookshops to nature trails. She frequently works with Maine Audubon, Liberty Graphics, park foundations, publishers and magazines. Jada is the creator of the popular *Home Tweet Home* window feeder, a decorated tiny home for birds. When not at her desk, Jada is bird watching or banding with a group of local ornithologists.

Visit Jada:

www.JadaFitch.com

www.facebook.com/JadaFitchillustration

Home Tweet Homes:

www.facebook.com/jadafitchbirdhomes

Other books by this illustrator

A Snowy Owl Story
Wildlife on the Move
Written by Melissa Kim
Illustrated by Jada Fitch
Islandport Press / Maine Audubon
2015

A Blanding's Turtle Story
Wildlife on the Move
Written by Melissa Kim
Illustrated by Jada Fitch
Islandport Press / Maine Audubon
2016

A Monarch Butterfly Story
Wildlife on the Move
Written by Melissa Kim
Illustrated by Jada Fitch
Islandport Press / Maine Audubon
2017

A Little Brown Bat Story
Wildlife on the Move
Written by Melissa Kim
Illustrated by Jada Fitch
Islandport Press / Maine Audubon
2015

www.ingramcontent.com/pod-product-compliance
Lightning Source LLC
Chambersburg PA
CBHW080831310526
45788CB00019B/3072